CONTENTS

D1634979

THE BEGINNINGS OF THE DEATH CAMPS

Nazism

BETWEEN 1941 and 1945, during the Second World War, about six million Jews were brutally murdered in Nazi-dominated Europe. This is what is meant by the term Holocaust.

Nazis were members of the National German Socialist Workers' Party developed and led by Adolf Hitler. Early in 1933 Hitler became the political leader, the chancellor, of Germany. The main opponents of Nazism were Socialists and Communists and Hitler immediately set about destroying these groups so that his own power would not be threatened in Germany. This was the beginning of the evidence of Hitler's long-term goal: to destroy or remove anyone who did not conform to his idea of the ideal state. The first camps created in Nazi Germany were concentration camps. These were prisons where Germans, who were identified as enemies of the Nazi state, were concentrated in one place for supposed 're-education'.

Hitler and his Nazi party had never made any secret of their dislike of Jewish people and their distrust of communism – in the mind of Nazis the rise of communism was seen as partly the fault

Left: On April 20, 1941 Hitler celebrated his 52nd birthday. In the same year, plans were made for the extermination of Jews in Nazi-occupied Europe.

Left: This Jewish family from Amsterdam prepare for deportation in the summer of 1943. The belongings they carried would have been taken from them on their arrival at one of the death camps in Poland.

of European Jews. To a Nazi, a Jew was doubly guilty if he or she was a Communist, but simply being a Jew was sufficient reason to isolate and deprive someone of his or her rights. Other groups, including homosexuals and Gypsies, were also hated by the Nazis because they were seen as being from an inferior race or a 'flawed' group of people. Along with Jews and Communists, homosexuals and Gypsies made up the prison populations of the first concentration camps.

The camp system was seen to be successful by the Nazis and developed and extended so that other types of camps (labour camps) were created. In 1939 the Second World War began when Great Britain responded to Hitler's invasion of Europe. After the war began, the Nazi's campaign of hatred against Jews reached a terrifying new level. This was the start of the Holocaust – the planned destruction of the Jewish people. Part of the overall plan to eradicate Jews involved the creation of special camps where Jews could be worked to death and systematically murdered – the death camps.

Concentration and Labour Camps

The first concentration camp was created at Dachau in Germany, in March 1933. It was established on the orders of Himmler who was the head of Hitler's paramilitary force, the Schutzstaffel ('protection squads'), known by its initials as the SS. A camp at Sachsenhausen, north of Berlin, was established the same year, followed by camps at Buchenwald and Flossenbürg. Another concentration camp, Ravensbrück, was also established as a women's prison.

The last of the major concentration camps to be established before the outbreak of war was at Mauthausen in neighbouring Austria. There were many ethnic Germans in Austria and Hitler himself came from one such Austrian family. Nazism had become very strong in the country and in 1938 Austria voluntarily accepted German rule. There were granite quarries near Mauthausen, and the SS set out to make money by using the prisoners of the camp as slave labour.

Below: In the years leading up to the outbreak of war in 1939, Joseph Goebbels, Germany's propaganda minister, was in charge of persuading the German people that Nazi treatment of Jews was justifiable.

Other countries in Europe were not willing to accept German rule, and responded to Hitler's ambition to dominate Europe by declaring war. The Nazis' reaction was to develop the labour camp, a second type of Nazi camp. Labour camps were first established in December 1939 for the purpose of contributing to Germany's wartime production. Like the concentration camps, they used slave labour – mostly prisoners of war and Jews.

Mass Murder

The occupation of Poland in 1939, with its population of three million Jews, brought Nazism to a new level of brutality. The consequences, especially for Jews and other minorities, were shattering. Some six million

Poles, nearly 20 per cent of the population of Poland, died as a result of Germany's conquest. The whole country was subjected to a ruthless operation to remove Jews from society. All Jews were ordered to gather and stay inside their traditional living areas, called ghettos, while the Nazis considered their options.

In 1941, two years after the outbreak of war, the Germans invaded Russia. This resulted in new, vast areas of land being occupied and civilian populations were at the mercy of Nazism. Special German forces, the Einsatzgruppen, had the task of seeking out and killing all those identified as enemies of the German state. In occupied countries this was the beginning of the organized killing of Jews. Many Jews were shot by Einsatzgruppen firing squads.

Below: Many Polish Jews were forced to do manual work for the Germans. At the end of a day's work, they returned to the ghettos where they were forced to live.

Mauthausen

W.J. Sacks, a prisoner who survived the Mauthausen concentration camp, described work in the granite quarry.

'It was notorious for the 186 steps which you had to climb at least seven times a day. And if that was not enough, an SS officer and a *Kapo* [a prisoner with supervisory duties] stood over us, the rocks were heavy, the sun burned our shaved heads mercilessly, and the gravel cut our bare feet. I went down with gastroenteritis, as we fell upon some cold water that had been stagnant so long it was green, and we drank it, ignoring the fact that we were being beaten on the back or pushed to the ground. I also saw the terrifying agony experienced by those dying of a twisted bowel. These wretches pleaded for death; the SS officer would laugh and say to them: "Using a bullet on you would be a waste of 18 pfennigs"; a few minutes later he would be shooting healthy people.'

(Quoted in Maria Hochberg-Mariañska and Noe Grüss, *The Children Accuse*)

The Einsatzgruppen began their executions of Jewish men – and in August 1941 this policy was extended to Jewish women and children too. Victims were mowed down by machine guns or shot individually – as many as 30,000 at a time – and buried in large pits which they had been forced to dig themselves.

During the second half of 1941 it became obvious to those Nazis directing this policy that the physical task of killing many thousands of people was becoming impractical. The psychological stress placed on the executioners, as well as the problem of what to do with the inhabitants of the now horrifically overcrowded ghettos, were added factors that led to the consideration of easier and more comprehensive methods of killing.

When Himmler visited Minsk on an inspection tour of occupied eastern Europe, he saw executions taking place for himself. He asked those in charge to devise other methods of killing. By the autumn of 1941, this research had led to experiments using the poisonous exhaust from trucks to gas victims.

Above: Two children, wearing armbands to identify them as Jewish, return to the Warsaw ghetto.

Below: The death camps were built by prisoners of war, Jews and other slave labourers.

The Death Camps

The decision to exterminate all of Europe's Jews was taken sometime around the middle of 1941. Up until this time Jews had been allowed to emigrate from Nazi-occupied Europe, but this now came to an end. The deportation of Jews to eastern Europe began in October 1941. 'The Jewish Question must be resolved in the course of the war, for only so can it be solved without a worldwide outcry', stated the German Foreign Office.

Many tens of thousands of Jews had died of starvation in the ghettos and had been executed on a large scale in Poland and Russia. But the

Right: Joseph Goebbels sits at Hitler's side. Like Hitler, Goebbels avoided being tried for his part in the war by committing suicide in 1945.

decision to prevent Jewish emigration from Europe and create special death camps for the murder of an entire race marks the beginning of the Holocaust (known as the *Shoah* in Hebrew).

Setting up the death camps was undertaken and organized in a highly professional manner. Only the better-established German firms with good reputations were consulted regarding the design and building of the crematoria that would have to dispose of thousands of corpses.

In January 1942, at Lake Wannsee in Berlin, a conference took place to finalize plans for the extermination of the Jewish race. Records of the meeting have survived and they conclude by saying that: 'Europe is to be combed from West to East in the course of the practical implementation of the Final Solution . . . The evacuated Jews will first be taken, group by group, to so-called transit ghettos, in order to be transported further east from there.' As a result of the Wannsee Conference, the Jews corralled in the ghettos now found their surroundings transformed into transit camps; their destinations the recently created death camps.

On 27 March 1942, Joseph Goebbels, Hitler's Minister for Propaganda, congratulated his regime's handling of the extermination of the Jews in his diary: 'No other government and no other regime would have the strength for such a global solution of the question.' The fact that the solution consisted of mass murder on an organized scale was left unsaid.

A letter from the Russian front

From a letter by Karl Kretschmer, a member of the SS serving in Russia in 1942, to his family back in Germany.

Sunday, 27 September
Dear Soska
I am feeling wretched and am in horribly low spirits. How I'd like to be with you all . . . I must pull myself out of it. The sight of the dead (including women and children) is not very cheering. But we are fighting this war for the survival or non-survival of our people . . . As the war is in our opinion a Jewish war, the Jews are the first to feel it. Here in Russia, wherever the German soldier is, no Jew remains.

(Quoted in E. Klee, W. Dressen & V. Riess, *Those were the Days*)

The Camp System

The extent of the camp system as a whole is astonishing. Most camps were small-scale labour camps, and at the height of the Second World War there were over 10,000 of these in total, mostly in eastern Europe. There were around 50 concentration camps, and six dedicated death camps: Auschwitz, Chelmno, Belzec, Majdanek, Sobibor and Treblinka (see map on page 13).

All the camps – the concentration camps, the ghettos, the labour camps, and the specialist death camps – shared basic characteristics. They were institutions to house prisoners on a long-term basis and they were not governed by ideas of legal regulations, unlike ordinary prisons. The camps became the means for carrying out the Holocaust. This was obviously so in the case of the specialist death camps, but many of the other camps were used to deliberately mistreat and work Jewish prisoners to death. In this sense, the distinction between the dedicated death camps and some of the other camps becomes blurred. At Mauthausen concentration camp, for example, the death rate for Jews reached 100 per cent.

Opposite: Inmates of a concentration camp march through a town to their work duties.

Below: The harsh climate of eastern European winters, combined with an inadequate diet and hard physical labour, killed many camp prisoners.

Chronology

1933	**January**	Hitler appointed German Chancellor
	March	First concentration camp at Dachau set up
1935	**Spring**	Nazis organize attacks on Jews and Jewish shops
1938	**November**	Jews forbidden to visit places of entertainment and expelled from schools. Jewish businesses closed down
1939	**September**	Start of Second World War
		Ghettos created in Poland
1941	**April**	German army high command agree to SS units operating alongside army units in Russia
	June	Germany invades Russia
	July	High-ranking Nazis begin working on the Final Solution
	September	Experiments gassing prisoners at Auschwitz
	December	Start of gassing Jews at Chelmno camp
1942	**January**	Wannsee Conference confirms arrangements for the Final Solution
	March	Gassing begins at Belzec
	May	Start of large-scale gassings at Auschwitz

HOW THE CAMPS WORKED

Worked to death

THE FIRST camps, as we have seen, were established to punish and 're-educate' political prisoners soon after the Nazis came to power. Within a few years, political opposition to Nazism had been effectively destroyed within Nazi-occupied Europe. The SS began to exploit some of the concentration camps as a source of free labour, by creating their own building materials industry. Buchenwald and Sachsenhausen were both close to deposits of clay and loam which could be used to make bricks. In 1938 Himmler founded the German Earth and Stone Works to set up the operation as a proper profit-making business. The brick-making factory near Sachsenhausen became the largest of its kind in the world, but the wealth being produced did nothing to improve the quality of life in the camps. The opposite happened, because profits could be maximized by working the prisoners to death before replacing them with new prisoners.

An inmate of Buchenwald, who survived the harsh life of working in the loam pits, described the cost in human terms: 'Every night saw its procession of dead and injured, trundled into camp on wheelbarrows and stretchers . . . The mistreatment was indescribable – stonings, beatings, 'accidents', deliberate hurlings into the pit, shooting, and every imaginable form of torture.'

The SS had grown from a small force set up to defend the Nazi party, into the most powerful organization in Germany. It was able to negotiate directly with many of the large industrial companies that wanted to profit from a ready supply of cheap labour. This was a development that followed on from the success of early work camps like Mauthausen. These operations co-existed alongside a very different objective – the need to exterminate the Jewish race. Orders were received from Berlin to adapt some of the work camps so that they could contribute to the task of killing people. This is how a camp at Majdanek in Poland, which started out as a concentration and labour camp for Poles and Russian prisoners, also became a death camp at the end of 1941.

Below: Germans used the camp prisoners to help them in the war effort. These prisoners at Buchenwald camp are building a railway line to link the camp with Weimar in Germany.

Right: Little remains of the Majdanek death camp. This stone carving marks where the camp entrance used to be.

Below: There were concentration camps in Germany, but the six death camps were all situated in eastern Europe. Auschwitz's good rail connections helped make it the largest camp.

Four New Death Camps

In addition to Auschwitz and Majdanek, four other death camps became operational in Poland between December 1941 and the middle of 1942. At the Chelmno death camp new arrivals were driven into a nearby forest. They were gassed on the journey there by the van's exhaust fumes. The only prisoners who were not killed were those selected for digging graves and burying the dead. Gassing started there in December 1941, while it was March of the next year before gassing started at the Belzec camp.

Belzec was located in a remote forest area, but a railway line connected it to Lublin where there was a Jewish ghetto. Belzec was made of two camps, a reception area where Jews arrived and left their clothes and belongings, and a second area where three small gas chambers were built. A two-metre-wide path, just over 50 metres long, connected the two camps. This became known as the 'tube'. Like the camp as a whole, the 'tube' was enclosed by barbed wire and was the prisoners' route to their deaths.

Below: Many of the Jews deported from the Lodz ghetto, in Poland, ended up in the Chelmno death camp which was built near the city.

Right: This store room in the Majdanek camp was found when the Soviet forces entered the camp to liberate survivors. This was where the clothes of murdered Jews were sorted and sent back to Germany for distribution to German citizens.

In April 1942, 100 miles to the north of Belzec, the larger Sobibor camp opened as a death camp. Franz Stangl was appointed its commandant. After a few months he was moved to take charge of an even larger camp at Treblinka, 75 miles northeast of Warsaw. In *Shoah*, a documentary film showing first-hand testimonies from witnesses of the Holocaust, Franz Suchomel, an ex-guard of Treblinka, described how, 'Woven into the barbed wire were branches of pine trees . . . People couldn't see anything to the left or right. Nothing. You couldn't see through it. Impossible.'

Treblinka, Belzec and Sobibor, between them, received well over a million people – almost all Jews – who were killed as soon as they got to the camp. They began to build Treblinka in May of 1942, and by September a quarter of a million people had been killed in this one camp alone. There was a short delay in the autumn when larger gas chambers were constructed, but the exterminations soon resumed.

Bergen-Belsen

Bergen-Belsen was never a typical concentration camp. It was established in 1943 to house a special group of wealthy and influential Jews. The Germans thought they might be able to exchange them for Germans imprisoned by the British and Americans. The inmates of Belsen, as the camp has come to be known, had to work and survive on little food, but conditions were generally better than at any other camps and there were no gas chambers. In 1944, as the Russians began their advance into Europe, the Nazis started evacuating camps in eastern Europe. Belsen was flooded with starving evacuees from these camps, who were left there to die.

Auschwitz

In 1940 a decision was made to set up a new camp for Polish political prisoners and the place chosen was near the town of Oswiecim in southwest Poland. The German name for the town, which had important railway connections with other parts of Europe, was Auschwitz. Rudolf Hoess, a committed Nazi, first arrived at Auschwitz to take control of the new camp in April 1940. Thirty German criminal prisoners then arrived in May to start work building the camp. They were helped by 200 Jews rounded up from the local area.

This first camp which Hoess supervised, to be known as Auschwitz 1, remained largely a prison work camp for a variety of inmates, especially Jews and political prisoners. A large number of prisoners were killed here, but its primary function was as an administration centre for the reception of Jews deported from all corners of Nazi-occupied Europe. The first prisoners arrived in June. Shortly after, peasants living in local villages were expelled to create more room for the camps. An area, six miles by three, became prison property.

Below: Heinrich Himmler discusses plans with the German manufacturer Max Faust, for the massive I G Farben factory at Auschwitz.

Auschwitz Facts

Guards: some 7,000 guards were employed at various times

Victims: the number of people who died at the three Auschwitz camps between 1941 and 1944 is uncertain, but a commonly accepted total figure is in the region of one million

Auschwitz II:

Buildings: 200 wooden huts, each 100 feet by 30 feet

Daily population: from 30-40,000 to over 120,000

Gas chambers: four

Capacity: in the summer of 1944 the camp staff worked 24 hours round the clock, gassing half a million Hungarian Jews in less than two months

I G Farben plant at Auschwitz III

Employed: about 40,000 slave labourers

Survivors: less than 15,000 survived

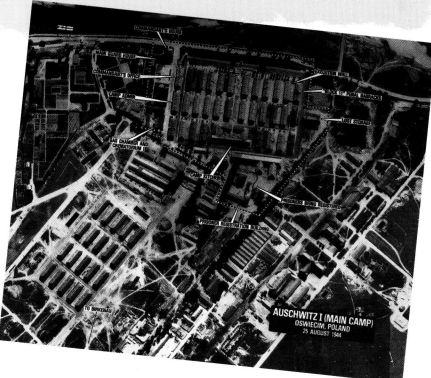

The planning of Auschwitz II began in late 1941. Building work started early the next year at a site some two miles away on the other side of the railway line, near a village called Birkenau in Germany. Birkenau underwent considerable development in the course of its existence and in the summer of 1942, when three gas chambers capable of holding over 1,000 people were ready for operation, plans were already being made for an extension.

Above: One of the aerial photographs of Auschwitz I taken by Allied planes secretly between April 1944 and January 1945.

Auschwitz III was another camp in the area. By the middle of 1942 it served as a slave-labour camp for a large German chemical and synthetic-rubber company, I G Farben. This was a large group of companies spread across Germany, and a special plant was established at Auschwitz to take advantage of the available slave labour. The labourers were mostly Jewish. Some were also forced to work as miners in two local coal mines which were taken over by I G Farben.

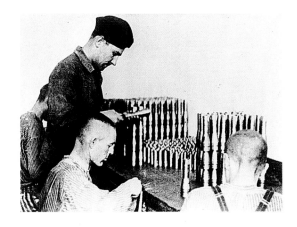

In addition, 50 smaller satellite camps that were dotted around the area developed. They employed slave labour. These included a cement plant, a steel factory, a shoe factory and a specialized camp where fuses were removed from unexploded bombs – dropped by the Allies in bombing raids over Germany. Auschwitz is the common name given to the three main camps as well as the various satellite camps.

Above: A German supervisor oversees slave labourers working in a munitions factory.

Below: Himmler inspects work on the I G Farben plant at Auschwitz in July 1942.

Above: Over 50 years on, Auschwitz's gates still stand as a reminder of all those who entered the camp, never to leave again.

In July of 1942 Himmler made an inspection of the Auschwitz camps to ensure that everything was going according to plan. He observed the process of killing, from when Jews first arrived off the trains up to the moment of their death. 'He made no remark regarding the process of extermination but remained quite silent,' remembered the camp's commandant. Before he left the following day, Himmler announced that he was satisfied with the camp's operation.

The origins of the Nazi's most infamous death camp as a work camp accounts for the three words that decorated the main gate to Auschwitz. Huge metal letters spelt out *Arbeit Macht Frei* – Work Sets You Free – a more ironic slogan for Auschwitz would be hard to imagine.

Who made the camps work?

In their different ways, Hitler and Himmler and other high-ranking Nazis and SS officers were all involved in making decisions that led to the construction of the camps. To make the camps work, however, meant the involvement of many thousands of people. The extent to which ordinary Germans knew about the Holocaust is a matter of debate. The author of a controversial study, *Hitler's Willing Executioners*, claims that most Germans supported the policy of mass murder, and that between 100,000 and half a million Germans were directly involved in the Holocaust. Other historians dispute this interpretation, arguing that the SS tried to hide the truth from ordinary Germans and that the majority did not support the mass murder of Jews and perhaps even did not know the scale of what was happening.

Holocaust Bonanza

Holocaust Bonanza is a deliberately offensive term that has been used by historians to describe the way in which both German and other international companies used slave labour from the concentration and death camps to increase their profits. More than 90 companies used slave labour at Buchenwald and 52 companies used Dachau. Fifty-one companies, including the Ford motor company's German operation, used slave labour from Auschwitz. Henry Ford, the founder of Ford motors, was an anti-Semite and he was a leading figure in the America First Committee which tried to keep the USA out of the war in Europe.

The I G Farben company, serviced by the labour of Auschwitz III, set up a main plant to produce synthetic rubber and a large-scale hydrogenation plant, designed to convert coal into oil. Those who ran I G Farben were businessmen, not necessarily Nazis. They saw the opportunity to increase their profits by entering into a commercial arrangement with the SS, whom they paid for an unlimited supply of cheap labour. The rate was the equivalent of $1 (60p) a day for a skilled worker, 75 cents (45p) a day for unskilled labour and, towards the end of the war, 40 cents (24p) for a child labourer. No money went to the prisoners, one of whom drew a comparison between his existence and that of the slaves of the ancient world: 'Only now do I realize what price was paid for building ancient civilizations . . . How much blood must have poured onto the Roman roads, the bulwarks, and the city walls.' To be fair to the Romans, they did place some value on their slaves. The Jewish labourers in camps like Auschwitz III had no value whatsoever and were freely worked to death.

Below: Anti-Semitic cartoons, like this one from 1936, were used by the Nazis to justify their treatment of the Jews and make ordinary Germans feel that the Jews posed a threat to their way of life.

As it turned out, I G Farben never made its planned-for profits because rubber was never produced and the hydrogenation plant was damaged by Allied bombing.

Left: Inmates of the Dachau camp in Germany contributing to the German war effort in 1943.

A policeman's excuse

'We had been drilled in such a way that we viewed all orders issued by the head of state as lawful and correct. We police went by the phrase, "Whatever serves the state is right, whatever harms the state is wrong." I would also like to say that it never entered my head that these orders could be wrong. Although I am aware that it is the duty of the police to protect the innocent, I was however at that time convinced that the Jewish people were not innocent but guilty . . . The thought that one should oppose or evade the order to take part in the extermination of the Jews never entered my head either. I followed these orders because they came from the highest leaders of the state and not because I was in any way afraid.'

Kurt Möbius, a policeman who served in Chelmno, testifying on 8 November 1961. (Quoted in E. Klee, W. Dressen & V. Riess, *Those were the Days*)

THE MECHANICS OF MASS MURDER

Murder by gas

Below left: A gas chamber reconstructed at Auschwitz I by the Polish authorities in 1948. Gassing actually took place at Auschwitz II.

DEATH by gas was first used for killing patients in hospitals and mental asylums after the start of the Second World War. Fake shower rooms were built in asylums, holding about 50 inmates, and carbon-monoxide gas was piped into them. Breakdowns in the machinery were common occurrences. Because these institutions existed in German towns with residential populations, there was also the problem of disposing of corpses without drawing attention to what was happening.

Below: Mass graves were dug and filled with the bodies of victims. Such graves were usually built close to the death or concentration camp.

The next stage was the development of gas vans, invented by German technicians. They devised a method of channelling a vehicle's poisonous exhaust fumes back in to its airtight interior. In theory, all the prisoners inside a van would be gassed while the vehicle drove to a burial pit in the countryside, but there were technical problems and sometimes there were still people gasping for air when the doors were opened. Sobibor, Belzec and Treblinka used diesel engines to supply the gas chambers with exhaust fumes.

In the summer of 1941, Hoess, the commandant of Auschwitz, was summoned to Berlin where he personally received orders

from Himmler to implement the systematic extermination of Jews in his camp. Auschwitz had been chosen, he was told, because of its size and isolation. Hoess then visited other camps in Poland to assess how they gassed their prisoners. He was looking for a method of killing to suit his camp. At Chelmno he learnt about the gas vans, the technical problem of distributing the gas evenly and the fact that relatively small numbers of prisoners could be killed by this method.

Zyklon B, a form of hydrochloric acid, had been brought to Auschwitz in order to exterminate rats and other vermin, as well as to disinfect the place. It was so effective that Hoess's deputy, Karl Fritzsch, decided to experiment with it on a group of 600 Soviet prisoners and hospital patients in September 1941. He discovered that Zyklon B proved equally effective in killing people as it did rats. It also killed people very quickly which meant more Jews could be killed in a day. This became the preferred method of extermination at Auschwitz.

The Language of Murder

At first, gas vans proved unsatisfactory because the van's large space meant that when it was filled with prisoners, referred to as 'merchandise' below, the vehicle's stability was affected by the heavy weight. A German engineer proposed reducing the size of the van's capacity. In this memorandum he deals with a possible technical problem:

'The manufacturers told us during a discussion that reducing the size of the van's rear would throw it badly off balance. The front axle, they claim, would be overloaded. In fact, the balance is automatically restored, because the merchandise aboard displays during the operation a natural tendency to rush to the rear doors, and is mainly found lying there at the end of the operation. So the front axle is not overloaded.'

(Quoted in Ronnie S. Landau, *Studying the Holocaust*)

The process of mass murder

Jews were gassed at all the death camps, but the process of mass murder at Auschwitz is better documented than at any of the other camps. It was the largest of all the camps and, once most of the Polish Jews had been exterminated, Germany used Auschwitz for the task of killing Europe's remaining Jews, Gypsies and homosexuals.

The first transport of Jews arrived there by rail in March 1942, before the gas chambers at Birkenau (Auschwitz II) were operational. Two more train loads arrived in April. Those not selected to work were gassed in an old barn and a farmhouse – up to 300 a day – while others were given lethal injections or shot. In time though, Auschwitz became a giant industrial concern, combined with a killing factory. Human beings were processed and destroyed as if on a production line at a factory.

After gassing, for hygiene reasons the corpses were hosed down by men in rubber boots wielding powerful hoses. The bodies

Below: Most of these women and children, photographed after getting off the cattle trucks at Auschwitz, would have been selected to go straight to the gas chambers.

In his own words

Hoess, the commandant of Auschwitz, described what happened in the 'shower rooms':

'The door would now be quickly screwed up and the gas discharged by the waiting disinfectors through vents in the ceilings of the gas chambers, down a shaft that led to the floor. This insured the rapid distribution of the gas. It could be observed through the peepholes in the door that those who were standing nearest to the induction vents were killed at once. It can be said that about one third died straightaway. The remainder staggered about and began to scream and struggle for air. The screaming, however, soon changed to the death rattle and in a few minutes all lay still . . . The door was opened half an hour after the induction of the gas, and the ventilation switched on.'

(Quoted in Jadwiga Bezwińska and Danuta Czech (eds), *KL Auschwitz*)

were then removed and taken to the crematoria and burnt in the specially-made ovens. The ovens had to be stoked up before cremation and hurriedly cleaned out afterwards, because there was always another batch of corpses waiting to be disposed of. Hoess described the problem at Auschwitz, 'Depending on the size of the bodies, up to three corpses could be put into one oven at the same time. The time required for cremation . . . took twenty minutes.' Operating at this pace meant that sometimes the system could barely cope, and there were delays caused by the failure of the crematoria that just couldn't keep up with the numbers of people arriving.

Above: This reconstructed crematorium is at Auschwitz. Parts of an original furnace were used in the reconstruction.

Streamlining murder

Mass murder at the camps was treated like a large-scale business, and one that could benefit from being organized in the most efficient way possible. Bearing this in mind, it made no sense to let the people know what was going to happen to them. They were already frightened by the experience of being rounded up and herded like cattle into trains. When the organized roundup of Jews from German-occupied Europe began in early 1942, victims were told they were being resettled in eastern Europe. To help convince them this was the case, they were told to bring their belongings and valuables with them for their new life.

Memoirs and interviews with Germans who worked in the death camps tell of the efforts that were made to deceive Jews into thinking they were not about to be murdered. The large, windowless cells in which they were gassed were made out to be showers, which in the interests of hygiene newly arrived inmates were to use before being assigned living quarters. At Sobibor, one of the SS leaders wore a white doctor's coat to give the impression that the showers served a hygienic purpose. At Treblinka, the commandant had a fake railway station constructed – with a painted clock and signs pointing to other destinations in Poland – as well as pointing to a restaurant and a

Below: Once the owners of these cases arrived at Auschwitz, they were never to see their possessions again. Some of the massive piles of goods, discovered by Russians liberating the camp in 1945, now form part of the exhibition for visitors coming to Auschwitz I.

ticket office. This was all to give prisoners the impression they had only arrived at a transit camp. Outside the 'shower room', pots of geraniums were placed to give a reassuring sense of normality.

Such tactics were very successful in Treblinka, where only about 20 SS soldiers and a force of 80 Ukrainians were needed to administer the killing process. At Auschwitz the large 'changing rooms', which could hold up to 1,000 people, had signs placed in various languages reading 'Baths and Disinfecting Rooms' and instructions to tie shoes together by their laces. Numbered pegs and coat hangers on the walls added to the illusion.

Attempts at deception did not always work and many people knew what was happening to them. Some people panicked, some tried to resist, many made efforts to comfort their children and act as normally as possible in an attempt to dignify their final moments together.

Above: This photograph of a liberated concentration camp in 1945 shows the dazed survivors surrounded by their dead companions.

Pigtail

A visitor to the Auschwitz musuem thinks about a display case with a huge pile of ·human hair found in a store room in 1945.

When all the women in the transport
had their heads shaved
four workmen with brooms made of
birch twigs swept up
and gathered up the hair

Behind clean glass
the stiff hair lies
of those suffocated in gas chambers
there are pins and side combs
in this hair

The hair is not shot through with light
is not parted by the breeze
is not touched by any hand
or rain or lips

In huge chests
clouds of dry hair
of those suffocated
and a faded plait
a pigtail with a ribbon
pulled at school
by naughty boys.

(*The Museum, Auschwitz, 1948* by Tadeusz Rözewiczin quoted from Hilda Schiff *Holocaust Poetry*)

Left: This crate of wedding rings was discovered by American troops when they searched a cave adjoining the Buchenwald concentration camp.

The spoils of murder

Part of the system of streamlining mass murder involved trying to make sure that absolutely nothing of any commercial value went to waste. Everyone, whether selected to live or die, was stripped of belongings upon arrival at a camp. Prisoners were carrying their most precious and essential belongings with them, so there was a vast amount of valuable goods that the German authorities expected to be sent to Berlin for processing. The process did not end with death. Before they were taken to the crematoria, the corpses of gassed Jews were checked for gold teeth – which were removed and collected in a bucket containing acid that would melt away flesh and bone. At the peak of its operation, a Jewish doctor at Auschwitz calculated that up to 20 pounds of gold could be collected over a period of 24 hours. The long hair of females was cut off in the same grisly manner and collected for various purposes, including the stuffing of pillows and making of socks for U-boat crews.

A Jewish prisoner who was forced to work in the crematoria spoke in the film *Shoah* of how, 'The Germans even forbade us to us the words "corpse" or "victim"… The Germans made us refer to the bodies as *figuren*, that is, as puppets, as dolls, or as *schmattes*, which means "rags".'

It was my job to shoot these people

From a statement of Will Mentz, known as 'the gunman' of
Treblinka:

'There were always some ill and frail people on the transports . . .
These people would be taken to the hospital area and stood or laid
down at the edge of the grave. When no more ill or wounded were
expected it was my job to shoot these people. I did this by shooting
them in the neck with a 9-mm pistol. They then collapsed or fell to
one side and were carried down into the grave by the two hospital
work-Jews. The bodies were sprinkled with chlorinated lime.'

(Quoted in Claude Lanzmann, *Shoah: The Complete Text of the
Acclaimed Holocaust Film*)

*Below: On arrival at Auschwitz,
these Hungarian women had
their heads shaved and were
given the thin uniform they
were to wear from then on.
They were separated from
their families and left to
wonder what their fates were.*

Genocide at all costs

By the beginning of 1944 the tide of the war had turned against the Germans. They were forced to face the prospect of defending their country from invasion from the east and the west.

The situation was critical for the Germans. But far from slowing down the slaughter of the Jews in order to concentrate on gaining ground in the war, efforts were redoubled to try and maximize the number that could be killed. At Auschwitz, the largest death camp, large-scale renovation work got under way. The heat from the ovens in the crematoria had caused cracks in the brickwork that needed repairing. The railway line was also extended to Birkenau, so that Jews no longer needed processing at Auschwitz I before being transported from there in trucks to the gas chambers. It was also decided to reinforce the chimneys of the crematoria and repaint the access area to the gas chambers.

The Nazis, after invading Hungary in March 1944, were determined to exterminate the country's entire population of Jews. The half a million resident Jews had their numbers swelled by another 300,000 who had fled there from other parts of eastern Europe in the hope of escaping persecution.

Below: Many methods of murder were used on those the Nazis wished to kill. These prisoners from the Buchenwald camp are lined up in a nearby forest, waiting to be shot.

By now, every train was needed to transport retreating German troops from Russia. But despite this, arrangements went ahead to use valuable fuel and trains to move Hungary's Jews to the waiting death camps. The machinery of murder worked overtime to bring some 400,000 to Auschwitz over a period of eight weeks, using three trains a day. To this day nobody understands the self-destructive and irrational stubbornness that prevented the Germans from trying to turn their fortunes around.

Below: Flowers lay by the Wall of Tears at Auschwitz where so many prisoners were shot.

I Keep Forgetting

I keep forgetting
the facts and statistics
and each time
I need to know them

I look up books
these books line
twelve shelves
in my room

I know where to go
to confirm the fact
that in the Warsaw ghetto
there were 7.2 people per room . . .

and how many
bodies they crammed
in Auschwitz
at the peak of production

twelve thousand a day
I have to check
and re-check . . .

and did I dream
that at 4pm on the 19th January
58,000 emaciated inmates
were marched out of Auschwitz

. . . I can remember
people's conversations
and what someone's wife
said to someone else's husband

what a good memory
you have
people tell me.

(*I Keep Forgetting* by Lily Brett, quoted from Hilda Schiff *Holocaust Poetry*)

DAILY LIFE AND DAILY DEATH

Selection upon arrival

For MOST inmates, the crashing sound of doors being opened on their transport train signalled their arrival at a death camp. After days spent cooped up in a sealed compartment, in which many had already died from exhaustion and suffocation, the moment of arrival brought short-lived relief. SS men in black uniforms, whips by their side and some with German shepherd dogs on tight leashes, barked orders and herded them into line. Experienced guards maintained an air of brisk efficiency, and anxious questions from terrified new arrivals were often dealt with by reassuring lies and promises. The idea was to maintain as calm an atmosphere as possible. As one woman survivor recalled: 'This is the greatest strength of the whole crime, its unbelievability. When we came to Auschwitz, we smelt the sweet smell. They [other inmates] said to us, "There the people are gassed, three kilometres over there." We didn't believe it.'

Below: On arrival at Auschwitz II, the inmates who escaped the initial selection were separated from their friends and families, shaved, stripped of all possessions and tattooed with a number.

The first procedure at a death camp usually took place as soon as everyone was off the train. The prisoners were lined up, and a process of selection followed, in order to decide who would be gassed and who would be chosen for work. The usual practice was for two SS doctors to be waiting on the platform as each trainload arrived and they very quickly waved each individual to the left – for the gas chamber – or to the right for work duties. A person's fate was decided on the basis of age and sex, with those over about 40 generally sent to the left, along with most women and children.

Below: This woman in the Bergen-Belsen concentration camp has typhus. The illness and suffering she has endured have aged her considerably.

Silent as an aquarium

In 1943 the 25-year-old Primo Levi, an Italian Jew, was deported from Turin to Auschwitz. He describes his arrival at the camp:

'A vast platform appeared before us, lit up by reflectors. A little beyond it, a row of lorries. Then everything was silent again. Someone translated: we had to climb down with our luggage and deposit it alongside the train . . . A dozen SS men stood around, legs akimbo, with an indifferent air. At a certain moment they moved amongst us, and in a subdued tone of voice, with faces of stone, began to interrogate us rapidly, one by one, in bad Italian. They did not interrogate everybody, only a few: "How old? Healthy or ill?" And on the basis of the reply they pointed in two different directions. Everything was as silent as an aquarium, or as in certain dream sequences. We had expected something more apocalyptic: they seemed simple police agents. It was disconcerting and disarming.'

(Quoted from Primo Levi, *Survival in Auschwitz*)

Processing

Even in a dedicated death camp like Chelmno, where only two men are known to have survived out of the 400,000 deported there, there was still a need to keep some alive for essential work duties. In the camp complex of Auschwitz, those who were not immediately selected for gassing were ordered to strip. Their hair was shaved and blue-and-white striped clothing was handed out to them, along with wooden clogs.

Men and women were divided before being lined up in alphabetical order so that they could be registered and tattooed on the forearm with a number. The numbering system was used to organize the daily allowances of bread and soup, and inmates who survived long enough learnt to interpret the numbers: those below 80,000, for example, represented early arrivals from the Polish ghettos. As well as the tattoo, inmates had a coloured triangle on their clothing to signify their status. Political prisoners had a red triangle, green for criminals, pink for homosexuals, and if a Jew fitted one of these categories a yellow triangle was placed on top to form a Star of David – the emblem of the Jewish people.

Below: Roll call took place twice a day. This photograph records a roll call at Sachsenhausen concentration camp.

Left: A camp survivor shows her tattooed number. She is wearing the Star of David to show that she is proud to be Jewish and in memory of those who died in the camps.

'From now on you're sixteen'

Elli Friedmann was 13 when she arrived at Auschwitz from Hungary with her mother, brother and aunt. Elli, who was not aware that anyone under the age of 16 was destined for the gas chambers, remembers a noisier scene.

'The column of women, infants and children begins to move. Dogs snarl, SS men scream orders, children cry, women weep goodbyes to departing men, and I struggle with my convulsive stomach . . . He [the man making the selection] looks at me with friendly eyes. *"Goldenes haar!"* he exclaims and takes one of my long plaits into his hand. I am not certain I heard right. Did he say 'golden hair' about my plaits?

"Bist du Jüdin?" Are you Jewish?
The question startles me. "Yes, I am Jewish."
"Wie alt bist du?" How old are you?
"I am thirteen."
"You are tall for your age. Is this your mother?" He touches Mummy lightly on the shoulder.
"You go with your mother."
With his riding stick he parts Aunt Serena from Mummy's embrace and gently shoves Mummy and me to the group moving to the right.
"Go. And remember, from now on you're sixteen." '

(Quoted in Livia Bitton-Jackson, *I Have Lived a Thousand Years*)

A day's routine

A day always began with a roll call before dawn. The process could take hours. Everyone was counted, even those who died during the night were propped up in position for the roll call. Then prisoners marched away to their work duties. There was a camp band in parts of Auschwitz that played march music to accompany the prisoners as they left for work each morning.

Auschwitz was largely self-sufficient and this meant that the nature of work duties varied a lot. Places like the bakery provided a relatively easy work assignment, but more common was the hard labour that went into building extensions and laying new roads for the camp. All work, whatever its nature, was hard to bear because of the meagre food allowances. Everyone was weak and the poor food rations made disease and illness very common.

A time that prisoners had to themselves was at night in their barracks or during the day at the latrines. Toilets usually

Below: Communal toilets were one of the few places where people could gossip, barter food and possibly get news of their family or the progress of the war. This one is inside, but many were ditches in the open. Lack of sanitation caused epidemics of typhus and dysentery.

consisted of a long wide ditch. Prisoners were escorted there by guards in groups of up to 50.

Below: In 1933, Dachau was paradise compared to the horrors of the camp after 1941.

Death was an inescapable part of daily camp life and prisoners did not pretend otherwise. They knew about the gas chambers and they discussed amongst themselves how long it probably took to die there. Fellow-prisoners were regularly dying of disease and weakness, or falling victim to the regular 'selections' that weeded out those no longer capable of working. Anyone failing a selection was taken to the gas chamber and killed.

Survival skills

Jean Amery, a prisoner at Auschwitz, explains how professional people like lawyers and journalists, lacked the necessary survival skills:

'Camp life demanded above all bodily agility and physical courage that necessarily bordered on brutality . . . Assume for a moment that we had to prevent a professional pickpocket from Warsaw from stealing our shoelaces. Circumstances permitting, an uppercut certainly helped . . . only very rarely did the lawyer or gymnasium teacher know how to execute an uppercut properly . . . In matters of camp discipline things were also bad. Those who on the outside had practised a higher profession generally possessed little talent for bedmaking. I recall educated and cultivated comrades who, dripping with sweat, battled every morning with their straw mattress and blankets and still achieved no proper results, so that later, at the work site, they were plagued by the fear – which grew into an obsession – that on their return they would be punished with a beating or the withdrawal of food.'

(Quoted from Jean Amery, *At The Mind's Limits*)

Surviving

For those not selected for immediate death, the single most important factor affecting a person's chances of survival was the kind of work he or she was assigned to. Food rations were barely enough to keep anyone alive for very long and heavy labour, especially in the coal mines, meant certain death. Prisoners who had a trade – for example a machinist, plumber, carpenter, electrician or cabinetmaker – stood some chance of an indoor assignment at one of the Auschwitz work camps. Businesspeople and professionals, like lawyers or teachers, had no useful skills that could be exploited, and they were more likely to be assigned to a short life of hard labour.

Left: An early photograph taken at Sachsenhausen concentration camp. The barracks are comfortable and the food rations generous in comparison with conditions at the camp towards the end of the war.

Towards the end of 1943 there were small but significant changes in life at Auschwitz. These changes increased the chances of survival for those not selected for the gas chambers. The reason for this is not clear, but it may have something to do with the growing realization that Germany was not winning the war and that people might be held accountable for what they were doing. The majority of prisoners in the work camps were not Jews but prisoners of war, and around the middle of 1943 the decision was made to stop gassing non-Jews. This, of course, made no difference to the fate of Jews who continued to arrive in large numbers.

Below: Belsen concentration camp after liberation in 1945. Bodies litter the sides of the road, while survivors stand around.

Canada

The personal belongings that Jews were stripped of when they arrived at camps did not always get processed in the intended manner. The sheer volume of people arriving at Auschwitz led to a building being used to store valuable goods. This developed into what has been called the largest black market in Europe. There was a vast trade amongst prisoners, kapos and the Germans. Just about everything was for sale – food, clothes, precious stones, carpets, shoes, even the gold bars made from the teeth of victims. The barracks where the goods were stored, and pilfered from by corrupt guards, became known as Canada. This was because many Poles had emigrated there before the war, and they had good memories of the country and its legendary prosperity.

Surprises at Auschwitz

The idea of a hospital at Auschwitz sounds a remarkable contradiction, but one did exist. The SS would have liked to gas everyone who was ill. They began removing patients to kill them, but prisoners stopped reporting illness. This increased the danger of infectious diseases spreading through the camp and possibly affecting Germans. The hospital became a sanctuary, even though there were still 'selections', where patients were simply dragged off to the gas chambers by SS guards.

The idea of a law court seems equally bizarre, given the simple fact that normal rules of justice did not apply in the camps. Prisoners, however, developed their own code of justice and certain offences, like stealing another prisoner's food or informing on someone, were dealt with at night in secret makeshift courts. Punishments took the form of lashes or even death for serious offences.

Perhaps the most astonishing thing to happen at Auschwitz was when an SS judge arrived in mid-1943 to investigate corruption at the camp. An SS guard had attempted to send home some stolen gold to his family. He had been discovered. The judge, Morgen, had already investigated financial fraud at the Buchenwald camp. The commandant there was prosecuted and executed as a result. Morgen brought charges against a high-

Left: Medical experiments were carried out on this dissecting table at Auschwitz.

ranking officer at Auschwitz who was put on trial in Berlin and imprisoned. German military authorities were keen to uphold standards of professional conduct, yet they were carrying out the largest act of mass murder the world had ever witnessed.

Auschwitz was full of macabre surprises. One such was the tradition of putting up a Christmas tree, decorated with coloured lights, close to one of the gas chambers. Most of the Germans who made Auschwitz work were practising Christians, and they selected prisoners who were forced to sing 'Silent Night'.

Caption: This room at Auschwitz was the 'punishment' room. Prisoners who disobeyed the rules were sent there.

Leave Us

Forget us
forget our generation
live like humans
forget us

we envied
plants and stones
we envied dogs

I'd rather be a rat
I told her then

I'd rather not be
I'd rather sleep
and wake up when war is over

Forget us
don't enquire about our youth
leave us

(*Leave us* by Tadeusz Rözewicz Quoted in Hilda Schiff, *Holocaust Poetry*)

PEOPLE IN THE CAMPS

The commandant

EACH CAMP had its commandant. These men were in overall charge of the organization and daily administration of camp life. The commandant of Sobibor and then Treblinka, Franz Stangl, was a practising Catholic with a family whom he was devoted to. Like others who were captured after the war and questioned about what they did, Stangl seemed to lack any sense of moral responsibility. 'That was my profession', he stated, 'I enjoyed it. It fulfilled me.'

The commandant about whom the most is known is Major Rudolf Hoess. He had gone into hiding after the war but was recognized, put on trial and executed at Auschwitz in April 1947. Hoess wrote an account of his time at Auschwitz after his arrest and, like Stangl, showed a startling unawareness of his inhumanity. 'I must emphasize here that I have never personally hated the Jews', he wrote. His report includes harrowing observations, like the fact that 'women who either guessed or

Above: SS Hauptaturmffuührer Josef Kramer, the commandant of Bergen-Belsen concentration camp in Germany.

Left: Camp commandants lived in comfortable accommodation close to the camp. This was the house of the commandant of the Belzec death camp in Poland.

'I deeply regret'

'My family, to be sure, were well provided for in Auschwitz. Every wish that my wife or children expressed was granted them. The children could live a free and untrammelled life. My wife's garden was a paradise of flowers . . . No former prisoner can ever say that he was in any way or at any time badly treated in our house. My wife's greatest pleasure would have been to give a present to every prisoner who was in any way connected with our household.

. . . In summer they [his children] splashed in the paddling pool in the garden, or in the Sola. But their greatest joy was when Daddy bathed with them. He had, however, so little time for all these childish pleasures. Today I deeply regret that I did not devote more time to my family. I always felt I had to be on duty the whole time.'

Rudolf Hoess, commandant of Auschwitz, writing from a Polish prison after the war.

(Quoted in Jadwiga Bezwińska and Danuta Czech (eds), *KL Auschwitz*)

knew what awaited them nevertheless found the courage to joke with the children to encourage them, despite the mortal terror visible in their own eyes.'

Hoess, like Stangl, was brought up in a religious family and his parents wanted him to become a priest. But the young man joined the army when he was only 16 and took part in the First World War. In the early 1920s he was sentenced to life imprisonment for involvement in a political murder, but was freed after five years under an amnesty. He joined the SS, gained promotion after working at Dachau and Sachsenhausen, and being noted by Himmler for his dedication to duty was put in charge of Auschwitz. He remained the overall governor, the commandant, of the entire Auschwitz complex in the course of its evolution into Germany's largest concentration and death camp. He lived there with his wife and their five children in a detached house. It was shrouded from the rest of the camp by a concrete wall.

Above: The young Rudolph Hoess, commandant of Auschwitz. In captivity after the war, before he was executed, he wrote a memoir trying to justify his actions during the war.

The SS

The SS came into existence in 1925 as a group of bodyguards for
Hitler, and when Himmler took control of the group four years
later there were less than 300 members. Himmler cultivated the
image of the SS as an elite force of superior Nazis. They wore a
black uniform that contrasted dramatically with the ideal type of
blond-haired and blue-eyed German that joined the organization.
By the time the first death camps were operating, the SS had
become a paramilitary force of some quarter of a million men.
From this private army men were allocated to organize and run
the system that administered the Final Solution.

Many of the 3,000 or so members of the SS who were quartered
at Auschwitz, in common with those at the other death camps,
received extra rations for participating in the gassing operations.
For many the real bonus was that their life was not in any
physical danger, unlike SS units assigned to active combat
situations. For high ranking officers there were many privileges.

*Below: These SS men and
police officials at Buchenwald
in Germany had an easy life –
extra rations, living close to
home and, unlike those sent to
the Russian front, little chance
of being killed in action.*

Above: Christmas celebrations at Oranienburg concentration camp in Germany at the end of 1933.

The Deciding Factor

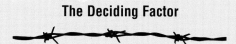

The SS soldier is popularly seen as a ruthless and sinister figure, but for Franz Hofmann, who served at Auschwitz, the reason for joining the SS was a very practical one.

'I would also like to say that my decision to enter the SS was made easier by the fact that it did not cost me anything. My brother, who later died on the Eastern Front, had previously been a member of the SS until he was expelled for some reason, so I was able to have his uniform and did not have to buy myself a new one. I would like to say today that I would certainly not have become a member of the SS if I had not been able to use my brother's uniform. The uniform was the deciding factor.'

(Quoted in E. Klee, W. Dressen & V. Riess, *Those were the Days*)

Kapos and *Muselmänner*

Those prisoners who survived the first selection process were destined for a gruelling life of hard labour. The Germans organized the inmates' workload by using prisoners to administer the system for them. The routine of daily life, like the lengthy morning roll call, was kept going by selected prisoners, known as kapos in camp jargon. They were responsible for day-to-day affairs. Kapos were usually non-Jewish Germans, either political prisoners or just criminals, and they answered to a small number of SS men. From a prisoner's point of view the kapos were powerful, and getting on the wrong side of them could spell disaster. One survivor called them the 'aristocrats of the camps'. Simple matters like the assignment of duties could be crucial, and if a kapo could be bribed or persuaded to assign someone to indoor work, this might be the difference between life and death.

The kapos' privileged position meant they had their own room in the barracks, but the SS guards could always demote them at a moment's notice and then they faced the wrathful revenge of the common prisoners.

While kapos were the most likely to survive in a camp, the least likely to survive were those whose strength of will gave way under the physical and psychological pressures. The camp jargon for these people was *Muselmänner* (Muslim men), from the mistaken idea that a Muslim's belief in fate meant a surrender of the will and a willingness to accept one's fate as inevitable. The term *Muselmänner* described those inmates who gave up believing they could survive, whose sense of self and will to live was crushed and broken. Their ordeal robbed them of any sense of control over their life. Considering the situation they were in, this was an understandable state of mind.

Opposite: Kapos, like this man who had killed Russians in front of their comrades, faced the wrath of former prisoners after the liberation of the camps in 1945.

Below: Kapos, like the men shown here not in the camp uniform, lived relatively privileged lives. They were usually German criminals rather than political prisoners or Jews.

Diary of an SS Officer

From the diary of Dr. Johann Paul Kramer, an SS officer who served in Poland in 1942.

September 6: Today an excellent Sunday dinner: tomato soup, one half of chicken with potatoes and red cabbage, and magnificent vanilla ice cream.

September 20: This Sunday afternoon I listened from 3pm till 6pm to a concert of the prisoners' band in glorious sunshine; the bandmaster was a conductor of the State Opera from Warsaw. Eighty musicians. Roast pork for dinner . . .

September 27: This Sunday afternoon, from 4 till 8, a party in the club with supper, free beer and cigarettes. Speech of Commandant Hoess and a musical and theatrical program . . .

November 8: . . . We had Bulgarian red wine and plum brandy from Croatia.

(Quoted in E. Klee, W. Dressen & V. Riess, *Those were the Days*)

The Sonderkommando

The Sonderkommando, the special command, were Jewish prisoners who had the most gruesome tasks of all in the death camps. Their job was to channel those selected for immediate death into the gas chambers with the minimum of fuss. They maintained the pretence that the prisoners were only having a shower, advising them to undress and pack their clothes carefully so that they could be collected afterwards. A Jewish doctor at Auschwitz described how, opening the gas chamber doors afterwards, the Sonderkommando stood equipped with their rubber boots and water hoses to wash down the bodies. After tying straps around the wrists of the corpses they dragged them out and into a nearby room. This room led to the elevators that could carry over 20 bodies up to the crematoria.

Opposite below: In September 1941, 33,771 Jews from Kiev were taken to a ravine outside the city of Babi Yar in the Ukraine and shot. This picture shows German policemen picking through the victims' clothes.

Another Sonderkommando team was waiting to remove the bodies from the elevator and feed them into the giant ovens. First though, they cut off and collected the hair of the victims and extracted any gold teeth. Sometimes people in the Sonderkommando team were selected because of their skills, like the dentists who were chosen for the task of extracting teeth from the dead prisoners.

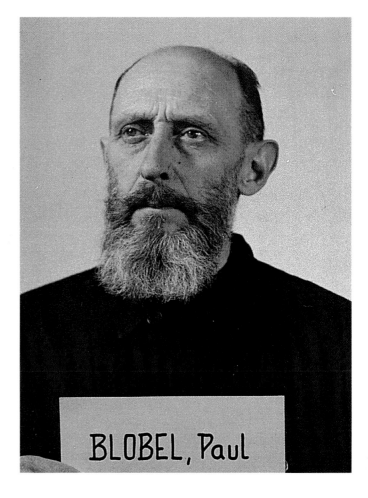

BLOBEL, Paul

Right: Paul Blobel was a commander of a special group responsible for the execution of thousands of Jews. He was sentenced to death at the War Trials in 1948.

'The competition'

'I estimate that the number of Jews gassed at Sobibor was about 350,000. In the canteen at Sobibor I once overheard a conversation between Frenzel, Stangl and Wagner. They were discussing the number of victims in the extermination camps of Belzec, Treblinka and Sobibor and expressed their regret that Sobibor "came last" in the competition.'

From a statement by Erich Bauer, a guard at Sobibor.
(Quoted in E. Klee, W. Dressen & V. Riess, *Those were the Days*)

The Sonderkommando, in a perverse and short-lived kind of way, could consider themselves lucky. While they were alive they enjoyed a better material standard of living than their fellow prisoners. One survivor has described how he arrived at the special barracks reserved for them and found a table laid for dinner with 'fine initialled porcelain dishes, and place settings of silver' (stolen from the luggage of Jews). The lifespan of a Sonderkommando was strictly limited and in time most of them found themselves being shepherded into the chambers by those selected to replace them.

Doctors

Doctors were not needed at camps like Sobibor and Chelmno, which were purely dedicated to exterminating Jews. But at Auschwitz they were employed to select those prisoners who seemed to be fit and healthy enough for slave labour.

Joseph Mengele is the most infamous of the various doctors who used the death camps as laboratories for medical experiments – unhampered by the normal restrictions of civilized life. Any organization or company in Germany could make a request to the SS central office in Berlin for an experiment. There is a record, for example, of the pharmaceutical company of Bayer requesting female prisoners to test out a new drug. Mengele,

Below: This Auschwitz survivor recieves treatment from a Russian doctor in January 1945.

whilst working at Auschwitz on a method of increasing the birth rate of Germans, was especially interested in the physical and genetic make-up of twins. So they were the only children who were not immediately selected for death. Investigations into methods of sterilizing Jews and other 'inferior' races involved experiments using radiation and injections of different formulae. Like Mengele's twins, victims who survived were usually gassed afterwards. The results of some experiments were written up and presented as scientific papers to doctors at conferences in Germany.

Survivors remember Mengele – his liking for white gloves and how he whistled themes from the operas of Wagner while making selections of newly-arrived prisoners.

Below: Joseph Mengele, doctor at Auschwitz between May 1943 and November 1944, murdered many Jews in the course of carrying out his brutal experiments.

'There was nothing I could do'

Maximilian Grabner was a high-ranking officer who administered the death camps. In a statement made after the war he gave this astonishing account of himself:

'To kill three million people is in my view the greatest crime of all. I only took part in this crime because there was nothing I could do to change anything . . . I am a Roman Catholic and today still believe in God. I believe there must be such a thing as divine justice as well as justice on earth. I only took part in the murder of some three million people out of consideration for my family. I was never an anti-Semite and would still claim that every person has the right to life.'

(Quoted in E. Klee, W. Dressen & V. Riess, *Those were the Days*)

THE END OF THE CAMPS

The end of Belzec and Chelmno

BY THE end of 1942, most of Poland's three million Jews had been exterminated. This meant that some of the death camps created mainly for this purpose were no longer needed, or could slow down their pace of gassings. Belzec camp was the first to close down its gas chambers, in December 1942. Auschwitz's size and efficiency made it possible to deal with the remaining Jews and other minorities who were to be wiped out.

The crematoria at Belzec were dismantled, the buildings burned down and cleared away and the remaining Jews shot. No trace remained of a camp where 600,000 people had been murdered.

Below: During the winter of 1942, the remaining Jewish prisoners at Belzec were shot. This woman waits to die.

By 1946 there were only two survivors of Belzec alive and one of them, Chaim Hirszman, was giving evidence in the nearby town of Lublin when he was murdered by Poles on his way home – because he was a Jew.

Below: A German officer stands by a lorry full of corpses as a British news team records his explanation of what happened.

Chelmno death camp did not begin to close down until the end of 1944. It took over two months for a remaining group of 100 Jews to dismantle the crematoria. By the middle of January 1945 there were 41 left alive. They were then taken out of their barracks one night in groups of five and shot. One prisoner was shot but not killed. He managed to survive, as did another one who managed to stab an SS guard and break his flashlight before escaping into nearby woods.

The last march

Giza Landau was 13 when she arrived at Auschwitz in late 1944 and she took part in the final forced evacuation of the camp:

'The Russians must have been very close by then, as the Germans were in a great hurry. We were not allowed to stop even for a moment, day or night. If someone bent over to straighten their shoe or have a rest, or if someone grew weak and could not keep up, they were shot on the spot. We marched down side-roads, through woods, in the snow. All along the way there were corpses, some of them even in a sitting position. I tried not to look but it was impossible to avoid them. After two days we were put into open wagons. There was no food whatsoever; there was no more bread, and we ate snow. No one believed any longer that they would survive.'

(Quoted in Maria Hochberg-Mariañska and Noe Grüss (eds), *The Children Accuse*)

Killings and uprisings

Such was the obsession with trying to kill as many Jews as possible, that even as it started to become clear that Germany's military defeat was only a matter of time, hastily organized executions began to take place. In less than one week in November 1943, 50,000 Jews were taken to Majdanek death camp and executed in front of ditches behind the gas chambers. At Auschwitz, even though the crematoria were now working 24 hours a day, the burning of corpses could not keep pace with the numbers being gassed – such was the determination to eliminate all the Hungarian Jews. To deal with this problem, huge pits were dug to accommodate up to 2,000 bodies which were then burnt together. The fires could be seen up to 30 miles away.

As the war drew to a close, uprisings took place in various camps. The prisoners realized they had a chance to escape and many of them preferred to try and escape, rather than wait for liberation. In August 1943 at Treblinka 150 escaped, killing 15 of the guards, though some of them were hunted down and shot. In October a planned revolt broke out at Sobibor, the password was 'Hurrah'. Three hundred prisoners escaped, though the same

Below: After the Sobibor uprising in 1943, about 300 prisoners fled into the woods. It is thought that about 60 of them survived the war, including this group.

number were shot by the guards. In the same month the Sonderkommando at Auschwitz rose in revolt, but the action was uncoordinated and only three SS men were killed while nearly all of the 700 Sonderkommando were shot.

Above: The remains of part of the vast Auschwitz camp still stand as a reminder of what happened behind those barbed-wire fences.

'How alive they were'

Fania Fenelon was in Bergen-Belsen when Allied troops liberated the camp.

'Our liberators were well fed and bursting with health, and they moved among our skeletal, tenuous silhouettes like a surge of life . . . They called to one another, whistled cheerfully, then suddenly fell silent, faced with eyes too large, or too intense a gaze. How alive they were; they walked quickly, they ran, they leapt. All these movements were so easy for them, while a single one of them would have taken away our last breath of life! These men seemed not to know that one could live in slow motion, that energy was something you saved.'

(Quoted in Martin Gilbert, *The Holocaust*)

Hiding the evidence: Majdanek, Treblinka and Auschwitz

As the Russians advanced westwards towards Poland it became obvious that the death camps would soon be reached. Himmler ordered the closedown of Majdanek camp and the evacuation of the remaining prisoners to Auschwitz, which lay further to the west. On July 24 1944, a Polish resistance group took control of the Majdanek camp and were there to meet the Russians when they arrived soon afterwards.

In late 1943 the equipment at Treblinka camp was dismantled by the remaining Jews, before they were shot in November. So complete was the removal of the camp that there was little left to indicate that 800,000 human beings had perished within the 60-acre plot of land called Treblinka. Sobibor was physically dismantled in the same way, with no evidence left of what had happened there.

The last victims died at Auschwitz on October 28, 1944. Within a month, the dismantling of the machinery of mass murder and the destruction of written records of what had taken place was ordered. Meticulous records had been kept, right down to falsifying death certificates for those gassed. In January 1945 when Auschwitz was being evacuated, the authorities tried to burn down Canada, the barracks packed with prisoners' belongings, but not everything was destroyed. The Russian

Below: This young person entered Auschwitz some time during 1943. When the camps were closed, all records, including this one, were to be burned, but many of them survived.

soldiers who first arrived were astonished to find amongst the ruins vast quantities of belongings: nearly 14,000 carpets, 38,000 pairs of shoes, 350,000 sets of men's suits and hundreds of thousands of women's clothes. Some of these items can be seen today at the museum at Auschwitz.

Left: This picture, called No Escape, by Moshe Galili shows a German executioner along with American, British and Russian soldiers. The painting implies that the Allies were guilty too, for not preventing the Holocaust, or stopping it sooner.

Buchenwald

In April 1945, on the day that Buchenwald was liberated, the American correspondent Edward Murrow made a radio broadcast describing what he saw:

'We went to the hospital. It was full. The doctor told me that 200 had died the day before. I asked the cause of death. He shrugged and said, 'TB, starvation, fatigue, and there are many who have no desire to live.'... [Another prisoner] showed me the daily ration: one piece of brown bread about as thick as your thumb, on top of it a piece of margarine as big as three sticks of chewing gum. That, and a little stew, was what they received every 24 hours.'

(Quoted in Louis L. Snyder, *Encyclopedia of the Third Reich*)

The Death Marches

By the middle of 1944 the victorious Russians were advancing towards Germany and the end of the Second World War in Europe was only a matter of time. In early 1945, remaining prisoners were evacuated and forced to march out of the death and concentration camps of eastern Poland. The SS wanted a slave labour force to build their final defences against the Allied armies. In January 1945 the Russians were close enough to Auschwitz to bombard parts of it with artillery, and the SS ordered the evacuation of the camp. The remaining Jews in Buchenwald were evacuated by the Germans in April. The injured and sick were left behind, and of the 60,000 who were marched off through the snow about 20,000 died along the way. The camp was liberated a week later, on 27 January 1945, and the Russian soldiers found the thousands of half-dead prisoners that had been left behind.

Around 10,000 of those marched out of Auschwitz, along with thousands of others evacuated from other camps, ended up in Bergen-Belsen concentration camp in Germany. British soldiers and tanks entered the camp in April 1945, after the Germans had left, and found thousands of unburied bodies – those who had died of starvation. Bulldozers had to be brought in to help bury them. Three hundred continued to die each day for a week and even two weeks later, when medical teams and food were well-organized, 60 people were still dying each day. One of those who died at Bergen-Belsen in the last weeks of the war was a young Jewish girl, Anne Frank, who had recorded her daily thoughts while hiding in a house in Amsterdam with her family, before her capture.

Below: American soldiers look on in horror at the victims who died in the final weeks of the Holocaust.

At Mauthausen camp, American soldiers were as shocked at what they saw as were the British at Bergen-Belsen. Thousands of half-dead prisoners were starving to death, and well-meaning Americans fed them with rich food like chocolate, which the prisoners' malnourished bodies couldn't digest. Many died as a result of this.

'How old do you think I am?'

'A middle-aged German woman approaches me.

"We didn't know anything. We had no idea. You must believe me. Did you have to work hard also?"

"Yes," I whisper.

"At your age, it must've been difficult."

At my age. What does she mean?

"We didn't get enough to eat. Because of starvation. Not because of my age."

"I meant, it must have been harder for the older people."

For older people?

"How old do you think I am?"

She looks at me uncertainly.

"Sixty? Sixty-two?"

"Sixty? I am fourteen. Fourteen years old."

She gives a little shriek and makes the sign of the cross. In horror and disbelief she walks away and joins the crowd of German civilians near the station house.

So this is liberation. It's come.

I am fourteen years old, and I have lived a thousand years.'

(Quoted in Livia Bitton-Jackson, *I Have Lived a Thousand Years*)

The Germans surrendered to the Allies in May 1945 but thousands of camp prisoners continued to die for many weeks afterwards. Their body weight reduced to less than 30 kilos (approximately the weight of a 7-year-old child), they had no strength or will left to live. Those who did recover their health were haunted forever by what they had lived through. There could be no happy ending for them, or for the millions of Jews and others who had died in the camps.

Above: By April 1945, the German concentration camps were being evacuated. These prisoners from Dachau are being forced to march to an unknown destination.

DATELINE

1933 **January** Hitler appointed German Chancellor
March First concentration camp set up at Dachau

1935 **September** New laws remove Jewish equality in the legal system and forbid marriage between Jews and non-Jews

1937 **September** Buchenwald concentration camp is established in Germany

1939 **September** Start of the Second World War
November All Jews in Nazi-occupied Europe had to wear a yellow Star of David
December All Jewish males between 14 and 60 are required for forced labour in labour camps that are established throughout Poland

1940 **October** The deportation of Jews to the Warsaw ghetto begins and a wall is built around the ghetto

1941 **June** Germany invades Russia
September Experiments gassing prisoners begin at Auschwitz
October Deportation of Jews to eastern Poland begins
December Start of gassing Jews at Chelmno camp

1942 **January** Wannsee Conference confirms arrangements for the Final Solution
March to October Deportation of Jews from France and Norway begins
March The first transports to Belzec, Majdanek, Sobibor and Treblinka get under way.
May Start of large-scale gassings at Auschwitz

September Start of large-scale gassings at Majdanek

1943 **January** Germans surrender at Stalingrad in Russia
April End of gassings at Chelmno
August End of gassings at Treblinka
October After the Nazi occupation of northern Italy, Italian Jews are deported to Auschwitz

1944 **May** Start of deportations of Hungarian Jews to Auschwitz
June Russians advancing westwards
D-Day: Allies land in northern France
Start of Death Marches
July Polish resistance take control of Majdanek and Soviet forces enter the camp
October Last victim gassed at Auschwitz

1945 **January** Evacuation of remaining prisoners from Auschwitz
Auschwitz liberated by Russians
April Bergen-Belsen camp and Buchenwald camp liberated by Allies
May Germany surrenders to Allies

Further Reading

Reg Grant, *The Holocaust: New Perspectives Series* , Wayland, 1997

Thomas Kenneally, *Schindler's Ark*, Hodder and Stoughton 1982

Clive A. Lawton, *The Story of the Holocaust*, Franklin Watts, 2000

Livia Bitton-Jackson, *I Have Lived a Thousand Years*, Aladdin Books, 1999

Hazel Rochman, *Bearing Witness: Stories of the Holocaust*, Orchard Books, 1995

Susan D. Bachrach, *Tell Them We Remember: The Story of the Holocaust*, Little Brown, 1994

Gerde Weissmann, *All But My Life*, Klien, Hill & Wang, 1995

Morris Wyszogod, *A Brush With Death: An Artist in the Death Camps*, State University of New York, 1998

Internet Sites

www.holocaust-history.org/
(This is a Holocaust History Project site)

http://remember.org/
(This is a cybrary, listing lots of other sites)

http://holocaustsurvivors.org/
(This site has stories from survivors and an encyclopedia)

Places to visit:

The Holocaust Exhibition, Imperial War Museum, Lambeth Road, London SE1 6HZ (Telephone bookings: 020 7416 5439; telephone enquiries: 020 7416 5320; recorded information: 0891 600 140). Not recommended for children under 14.

Holocaust Centre, Beth Shalom, Laxton, Newark, Nottinghamshire NG22 0PA (Telephone bookings and information: 01623 836627; email: office@bethshalom.com). Not recommended for children under 11.

Sources

The quotations in this book were taken from:

Jean Amery, *At The Mind's Limits*, Penguin, 1999

Jadwiga Bezwińska and Danuta Czech (eds), *KL Auschwitz*, Auschwitz Museum, 1972

Livia Bitton-Jackson, *I Have Lived a Thousand Years*, Aladdin Books, 1999

Otto Friedrich, *The Kingdom of Auschwitz*, Penguin, 1996

Martin Gilbert, *The Holocaust*, Collins, 1986

DJ Goldhagen, *Hitler's Willing Executioners: Ordinary Germans and the Holocaust*, Little, Brown & Company, 1996

Maria Hochberg-Mariańska and Noe Grüss (eds), *The Children Accuse*, Valentine Mitchell and Co, London, 1996

E. Klee, W. Dressen & V. Riess, *Those were the Days*, Hamish Hamilton, 1988

Ronnie S. Landau, *Studying the Holocaust*, Routledge, London, 1998

Claude Lanzmann, *Shoah: The Complete Text of the Acclaimed Holocaust Film*, Da Capo, New York,1995

Primo Levi, *Survival in Auschwitz*, Simon & Schuster, New York, 1996

Hilda Schiff (ed), *Holocaust Poetry*, St. Martin's Press, 1996

Louis L. Snyder, *Encyclopedia of the Third Reich*, McGraw-Hill, 1976

GLOSSARY

Allies countries that fought in the Second World War against Germany, Japan and their allies.

Anti-Semitism prejudice against Jewish people.

Auschwitz the largest and best-known Nazi camp in Poland, first established in 1941 as a prison labour camp. This original camp, which served as an administration centre for the whole Auschwitz complex, evolved into Auschwitz I and this is the part that has been preserved for visitors by the Polish government. The gas chambers and crematoria were built at another camp, Auschwitz II, about 6 miles away near a village called Birkenau. Auschwitz III was largely a slave labour camp for a nearby factory run by the I G Farben company.

Belzec a death camp in Poland that used gas chambers to murder around 600,000 Polish Jews.

Buchenwald a concentration camp established in Germany in 1938. In April 1945 all the Jewish inmates were forced out on a death march to another concentration camp further south. A short while later, American troops entered the camp.

Chelmno a death camp, established in western Poland at the end of 1941, that used gas vans to kill some 400,000 Jews who were deported there. It began to close down at the end of 1944 and the final prisoners were killed in January 1945.

Communism the theory that all property should be state-owned and that each person should be paid according to his or her needs.

Concentration camps large-scale prison and work camps, where prisoners were often worked to death but not in the systematic manner of the death camps.

Crematoria places where corpses are disposed of by burning.

Dachau the first Nazi concentration camp, established in March 1933 and liberated by American troops in April 1945.

Death camps also known as extermination camps, dedicated to systematically murdering their inmates, mostly Jews. All the Nazi death camps were in Poland: Auschwitz, Belzec, Chelmno, Majdanek, Sobibor and Treblinka.

Death Marches the forced evacuation of camp prisoners during the last stages of the war. Many thousands of the prisoners died or were murdered on these marches.(Some were also labour/concentration camps.)

Deportation to remove people by force to another country, as in the Nazi deportations of Jews from western Europe to death, concentration and labour camps in Poland.

Einsatzgruppen special units ordered to eliminate enemies of the state and mainly responsible for the mass killing of Jews and communists in occupied Poland and Russia.

Extermination complete destruction (of a race or species.)

Final Solution from the Nazi term, 'Endlösung'. The phrase 'Final Solution of the Jewish Question' was used when referring to the extermination of all European Jews.

Führer the German word for 'leader' and part of the title assumed by Hitler in 1934.

Genocide deliberate destruction of a racial, religious, political or ethnic group.

Ghettos the poorest districts in some European towns, where Nazis forced Jews to live and from where they were transported to death camps.

Goebbels, Joseph Hitler's Minister for Propaganda who was responsible for anti-

Semitic campaigns and was in charge of the deportation of Jews from Germany. In April 1945 he committed suicide in Hitler's bunker in Berlin, rather than be captured by the Allies.

Himmler, Heinrich head of the SS and organizer of the Final Solution.

Hitler, Adolf leader of the Nazi party and of Germany from 1933 to 1945; obsessive anti-Semitic.

Hoess, Rudolf commandant of Auschwitz; hanged by the Polish in 1947.

Holocaust term used since the Second World War to refer to the murder of some six million Jews.

Kapos selected prisoners, put in charge of ordinary prisoners, who managed many of the daily routines of camp life.

Labour camps camps using slave labour, mostly prisoners of war and Jews, to increase Germany's wartime production.

Majdanek originally a labour camp in Poland, Majdanek became a death camp with gas chambers at the end of 1941. Soviet forces entered the camp in July 1944 and Allied journalists and photographers recorded the genocide that had taken place there.

Mauthausen a concentration camp established in Austria before war broke out in 1939. Prisoners at Mauthausen were used as slave labour for nearby granite quarries that were owned by the SS.

Mengele, Joseph an infamous doctor at Auschwitz who selected prisoners for the gas chambers and conducted medical experiments on prisoners.

Muselmänner camp jargon for prisoners who lost the will to survive.

Nazi Party (Nationalsozialistische Deutsche Arbeiterpartei) in English 'National Socialist German Workers' Party'. Led

by Hitler, the Nazi Party governed Germany between 1933 and 1945.

Paramilitary a group with military training and structure trained for a specific job.

Shoah Hebrew for Holocaust.

Sobibor a death camp in Poland that began operating in April 1942 when around 250,000 Jews were gassed to death. In October 1943 a planned revolt broke out at Sobibor and about 300 inmates managed to escape.

SS (Schutzstaffel) in English 'protection squads'. Originally used as bodyguards to protect senior members of the Nazi Party, the SS developed into its most powerful organization and was responsible for controlling the concentration and death camps.

Sonderkommando special group of prisoners who were given tasks to carry out within the camps and who received certain privileges.

Stangl, Franz commandant of Sobibor and Treblinka death camps. Extradited from Brazil in 1967, sentenced to life imprisonment by a German court and died soon afterwards.

Treblinka a death camp established in Poland in 1942. Around 800,000 Jews perished in Treblinka before 150 prisoners broke out and escaped in August 1943. Before the end of that year, the camp was dismantled so that no evidence of its function would be found.

Wannsee Conference an important meeting that took place outside Berlin at Lake Wannsee in January 1942. The conference was about working out exactly how the Germans would carry out their decision to exterminate all the Jews living in Nazi-occupied Europe.

INDEX